Woman's Day

Tuesday Night is
Pasta Night

The Eat-Well Cookbook of Meals in a Hurry

Woman's Day

Tuesday Night is Pasta Night

The Eat-Well Cookbook of Meals in a Hurry

filipacchi
publishing

Contents

✳

CHEESE & VEGETABLES • 62

CREDITS • 96

Pasta Cacciatore

CHICKEN BREASTS · SERVES 6 · TOTAL TIME: 30 MIN

3 Tbsp olive oil

1 lb skinless, boneless chicken breasts, cut in bite-size pieces

¾ tsp salt

12 oz short fusilli or cellentani pasta

1 medium onion, chopped

1 large yellow bell pepper, cut in ¾-in. pieces

1 pkg (10 oz) sliced mushrooms

1 Tbsp minced garlic

¾ tsp dried Italian seasoning

¼ tsp crushed red pepper flakes

1 can (14.5 oz) diced tomatoes in sauce

1 cup mixed marinated olives, pitted and halved

⅓ cup chopped parsley

GARNISH: shredded Parmesan cheese

1. Bring a large pot of lightly salted water to a boil.

2. Meanwhile, heat 2 Tbsp oil in a large skillet over medium-high heat. Sprinkle chicken with ¼ tsp salt. Add to skillet and sauté 2 to 3 minutes until lightly browned, but not fully cooked. Remove to a plate.

3. Stir pasta into boiling water; cook as package directs.

4. Meanwhile, add remaining 1 Tbsp oil, the onion, bell pepper, mushrooms, garlic, seasoning, red pepper flakes and remaining ½ tsp salt to skillet. Cook, stirring often, 5 minutes, or until liquid evaporates and vegetables begin to brown. Add ¾ cup cooking water from pasta pot to skillet. Stir in tomatoes and olives. Bring to a simmer and cook, uncovered, 8 minutes.

5. Drain pasta. Add parsley and chicken to skillet and simmer 2 to 3 minutes or until chicken is cooked through. Return pasta to pot, add chicken sauce and toss to coat. Serve with shredded Parmesan cheese.

PER SERVING: 480 cal, 27 g pro, 55 g car, 4 g fiber, 17 g fat (2 g sat fat), 44 mg chol, 1,586 mg sod

Penne with Chicken, Asparagus & Lemon Alfredo Sauce

CHICKEN TENDERS • SERVES 6 • TOTAL TIME: 25 MIN

1 lb penne rigate (see FYI) pasta

1 lb thin asparagus, woody ends trimmed, spears cut in 1½-in.-long pieces

SAUCE

12 oz chicken tenders, cut diagonally in ½-in.-wide strips

½ tsp salt

½ cup flour

1½ Tbsp olive oil

1 jar (16 oz) Alfredo sauce

1 Tbsp grated lemon peel

3 Tbsp fresh lemon juice

¼ cup grated Parmesan cheese

1 large tomato, halved, seeded and diced

¼ cup snipped fresh chives

Freshly ground black pepper, to taste

GARNISH: finely shredded lemon peel

1. Cook pasta in a large pot of lightly salted boiling water as package directs, adding asparagus 3 minutes before pasta is done.

2. Meanwhile, sprinkle chicken with salt, then toss with flour to lightly coat.

3. Heat oil in a large nonstick skillet over high heat. Add chicken; sauté 3 minutes until golden and just barely cooked through. Add Alfredo sauce, peel, juice and cheese. Bring to a simmer and cook 1 to 2 minutes until chicken is done.

4. Drain pasta and asparagus; return to pot. Immediately add sauce, tomato, chives and pepper. Toss to mix and coat. Sprinkle with lemon peel.

PER SERVING: 576 cal, 29 g pro, 73 g car, 3 g fiber, 14 g fat (7 g sat fat), 86 mg chol, 1,192 mg sod

FYI Penne rigate is penne with ridges.

Rigatoni Primavera with Chicken

COOKED CHICKEN • SERVES 4 • TOTAL TIME: ABOUT 20 MIN

12 oz rigatoni pasta

2 Tbsp olive oil

1 bag (9 oz) fresh California stir-fry vegetables

1 pkg (10 oz) cooked chicken strips

1 Tbsp chopped garlic

1 cup chicken broth

½ cup grated Parmesan cheese

¼ cup fresh basil, cut into thin strips

1. Cook pasta in a large pot of lightly salted boiling water as package directs, reserving 1 cup cooking water before draining.

2. Meanwhile, heat olive oil in a large nonstick skillet over medium-high heat. Add stir-fry vegetables and cooked chicken strips; sauté 2 minutes.

3. Add chopped garlic; cook 1 minute. Stir in chicken broth. Reduce heat, cover and simmer 3 minutes or until vegetables are just tender.

4. Toss with drained pasta, grated Parmesan cheese, fresh basil and reserved cooking water as needed.

PER SERVING: 546 cal, 33 g pro, 71 g car, 4 g fiber, 14 g fat (4 g sat fat), 48 mg chol, 971 mg sod

FYI Rigatoni are short, grooved tubes.

Ravioli Soup

4 cans (14.5 oz each) 99% fat-free roasted garlic-seasoned chicken broth

1 bag (16 oz) fresh broccoli florets, halved if large

1 pkg (7 oz) refrigerated fresh mini beef ravioli

GARNISH: grated Parmesan cheese

1. Bring broth plus 1 cup water to a boil in a 4-qt pot. Add broccoli, reduce heat and simmer 4 minutes.

2. Add ravioli, bring to a simmer and cook, stirring occasionally, 5 minutes or until broccoli and ravioli are tender. Sprinkle each serving with grated Parmesan cheese.

PER SERVING: 214 cal, 9 g pro, 38 g car, 5 g fiber, 3 g fat (1 g sat fat), 21 mg chol, 1,809 mg sod

Penne with Tuscan Kale

CHICKEN BROTH • SERVES 4 • TOTAL TIME: ABOUT 22 MIN

12 oz penne pasta

3 tsp olive oil (preferably extra-virgin)

¼ cup pine nuts

1½ Tbsp minced garlic

1½ cups fat-free chicken broth

1 bag (1 lb) kale leaves, stems removed and coarsely chopped

¼ cup golden raisins

GARNISH: shaved Parmesan cheese and crushed red pepper flakes

1. Cook pasta in a large pot of lightly salted boiling water as package directs.

2. Meanwhile, heat 1 tsp olive oil, in a large nonstick skillet over medium heat. Stir in pine nuts; sauté 1 minute or until lightly toasted. Remove and reserve.

3. Heat 2 tsp olive oil in same skillet. Add minced garlic; sauté 30 seconds until aromatic. Add chicken broth, kale and golden raisins. Cover and steam 5 to 6 minutes until greens are tender.

4. Drain pasta and return to pot; toss with kale mixture and pine nuts. Serve with Parmesan cheese and red pepper flakes.

PER SERVING: 467 cal, 17 g pro, 80 g car, 4 g fiber, 10 g fat (1 g sat fat), 0 mg chol, 270 mg sod

Penne with Asparagus & Chicken Sausage

CHICKEN SAUSAGE • SERVES 6 • TOTAL TIME: 35 MIN

3 Tbsp olive oil

1 bunch asparagus (about 1¼ lb), cut diagonally in 2-in. pieces

12 oz fully-cooked chicken sausage, sliced

¾ tsp salt

1 lb penne pasta

1 cup frozen green peas

1 medium onion, finely chopped

1 cup shredded carrots

1 can (14.5 oz) diced tomatoes in thick juice

1½ tsp salt-free seasoning blend

¾ cup half-and-half

½ cup grated Parmesan cheese

1. Bring a large pot of lightly salted water to a boil.

2. Meanwhile, heat 2 Tbsp oil in large skillet over medium-high heat. Add asparagus, sausage and ¼ tsp salt. Cook, stirring often, 5 to 6 minutes until asparagus are crisp-tender. Remove to a plate.

3. Stir pasta into boiling water; cook as package directs, stirring in peas for last 4 minutes of cooking time.

4. Meanwhile, add remaining 1 Tbsp oil, the onion and carrots to skillet. Sauté over medium heat 3 minutes or until onion softens. Add tomatoes, seasoning blend and remaining ½ tsp salt. Add ½ cup cooking water from pasta pot to skillet. Cover and simmer 8 minutes.

5. Drain pasta. Add asparagus mixture and half-and-half to skillet. Simmer 2 minutes or until hot. Return pasta to pot. Add sauce and Parmesan cheese; toss to mix.

PER SERVING: **590 cal, 33 g pro, 74 g car, 5 g fiber, 18 g fat (6 g sat fat), 61 mg chol, 1,224 mg sod**

Easy Lasagna

TURKEY MEATBALLS • SERVES 6 • TOTAL TIME: 1 HR 10 MIN

❋

1 jar (26 oz) marinara sauce

1 can (14.5 oz) diced tomatoes with Italian herbs

1 tub (15 oz) part-skim ricotta cheese

½ cup plus 2 Tbsp grated Parmesan cheese

1 large egg

¼ cup chopped fresh basil

¼ tsp pepper

1 box (8 oz) no-boil lasagna noodles

3½ cups (12 oz) shredded mozzarella cheese

1 pkg (24 oz) fully cooked turkey meatballs, coarsely chopped

1. Preheat oven to 375°F. Have a 13 x 9-in. baking dish ready. Mix marinara sauce and diced tomatoes in a medium bowl. In another bowl, mix ricotta cheese, ½ cup Parmesan cheese, the egg, basil and pepper.

2. Spread ½ cup sauce over bottom of baking dish. Put 3 noodles crosswise, not overlapping, on sauce. Drop 3 Tbsp ricotta mixture down center of each noodle and spread to cover noodles. Sprinkle evenly with 1 cup mozzarella and about 1⅓ cups chopped meatballs. Spoon 1 cup sauce evenly over top.

3. Repeat layering noodles, ricotta, mozzarella, meatballs and sauce twice. Top with remaining 3 noodles, remaining sauce, mozzarella and the 2 Tbsp grated Parmesan cheese. Cover with nonstick foil or foil coated with cooking spray.

4. Bake 50 to 60 minutes until hot and bubbly, removing foil for last 10 minutes. Let stand 10 minutes before serving.

PER SERVING: 713 cal, 44 g pro, 61 g car, 5 g fiber, 34 g fat (16 g sat fat), 161 mg chol, 1,857 mg sod

There's no meat to brown or noodles to boil, and it can be assembled a day ahead.

Baked Rigatoni with Mini Turkey Meatballs

TURKEY MEATBALLS · SERVES 4 · TOTAL TIME: ABOUT 55 MIN

8 oz rigatoni pasta

1 jar (32 oz) fat-free tomato pasta sauce

18 refrigerated fully cooked appetizer-size turkey meatballs (from a 24-oz pkg)

1 tub (15 oz) part-skim ricotta cheese

½ cup grated Parmesan cheese

GARNISH: thin strips basil leaves

1. Cook pasta in a large pot of lightly salted boiling water as package directs; drain well. Preheat oven to 375°F. Have a 2½-qt casserole ready.

2. Toss pasta, sauce and meatballs in a large bowl to mix. Spread ½ in the casserole; top with dollops of ½ the ricotta, then sprinkle with ½ the Parmesan cheese. Repeat layers once. Cover with lid or foil.

3. Bake 35 minutes or until hot and edges bubble. Garnish with basil.

PER SERVING: 610 cal, 38 g pro, 77 g car, 6 g fiber, 18 g fat (9 g sat fat), 77 mg chol, 1,358 mg sod

Bow-Ties Marinara with Meatballs

TURKEY MEATBALLS • SERVES 4 • TOTAL TIME: ABOUT 20 MIN

12 oz bow-ties (farfalle) pasta

1 bag (6 oz) baby spinach

1½ cups marinara sauce

2 Tbsp balsamic vinegar

1 pkg (24 oz) appetizer-size cooked turkey meatballs

1 cup diced fresh mozzarella

1. Cook pasta in a large pot of lightly salted boiling water as package directs, stirring in baby spinach just before pasta is done.

2. Meanwhile, heat the marinara sauce, balsamic vinegar and turkey meatballs in a medium saucepan over medium heat, stirring occasionally, until hot.

3. Drain pasta and spinach, return to pot and add marinara mixture. Toss with fresh mozzarella.

PER SERVING: **821 cal, 52 g pro, 84 g car, 9 g fiber, 28 g fat (9 g sat fat), 152 mg chol, 1,649 mg sod**

Lasagna Rolls

TURKEY SAUSAGE · MAKES 12 · PREP: 25 MIN · COOK: 10 MIN · BAKE: 45 MIN

1 small onion, coarsely chopped

1 small carrot, coarsely chopped

3 links (about 8 oz) Italian turkey sausage

2 tsp minced garlic

½ tsp *each* salt and fennel seeds, crushed

2¼ cups (8 oz) frozen cut leaf spinach, thawed and squeezed dry

1 cup part-skim ricotta cheese

⅓ cup grated Parmesan cheese

8 oven-ready lasagna noodles (from an 8- or 9-oz box)

2½ cups bottled marinara sauce

¾ cup chicken broth

PLANNING TIP Can be prepared through Step 6 up to two days ahead. Cover with plastic wrap, then foil; refrigerate. To bake, remove plastic wrap and cover with foil.

1. Have ready a 9 x 5-in. loaf pan and a 13 x 9-in. baking dish.

2. Put onion and carrot in food processor and pulse until finely chopped. Remove sausage from casing, add to processor and pulse until well blended.

3. Heat a large nonstick skillet over medium heat; coat with cooking spray. Add sausage mixture and cook 5 to 7 minutes, breaking up clumps, until no longer pink. Add garlic, salt and fennel seeds; cook 3 minutes, or until garlic is fragrant. Transfer to a bowl; let cool slightly. Add spinach, ricotta and Parmesan cheese; stir until well blended.

4. Fill loaf pan with hot water. Add noodles 1 at a time. Let soak 8 to 10 minutes until soft.

5. Mix marinara sauce and chicken broth in the baking dish.

6. To ASSEMBLE: Place a paper towel on work surface. Remove 2 lasagna noodles from water and place on towel, end to end, overlapping by ¾ in. Spread ¼ of the sausage mixture (about ¾ cup) on noodles leaving ¾ in. at one end. Beginning at other end, roll up. Cover with a damp paper towel to keep roll moist. Repeat with remaining noodles and sausage mixture. Cut each roll crosswise in thirds. Place cut sides up in sauce in baking dish.

7. Heat oven to 375°F. Bake 45 minutes, or until hot and bubbly.

PER SERVING (2 ROLLS): **326 cal, 19 g pro, 37 g car, 4 g fiber, 13 g fat (5 g sat fat), 36 mg chol, 1,370 mg sod**

Philly Cheesesteak Pasta

SIRLOIN STEAK • SERVES 4 • TOTAL TIME: 25 MIN

8 oz gemelli or rotelle pasta

2 cups milk

2 Tbsp cornstarch

1 Tbsp Dijon mustard

¼ tsp paprika

1 cup shredded reduced-fat Cheddar cheese

1½ cups cooked sirloin steak, cut in narrow strips

1 cup sautéed onions, chopped

1 cup diced tomatoes

GARNISH: chopped parsley

1. Cook pasta in a large pot of lightly salted boiling water as package directs. When pasta is done, drain and return to pot. Meanwhile, whisk milk and cornstarch in a medium saucepan to blend. Bring to a boil over medium-high heat, stirring often.

2. Whisk mustard and paprika into milk; simmer 1 minute or until thickened. Add cheese, steak and onions; stir until cheese melts. Remove from heat; toss with pasta in pasta pot. Top with the tomatoes; sprinkle with parsley.

PER SERVING: **496 cal, 35 g pro, 57 g car, 3 g fiber, 13 g fat (7 g sat fat), 79 mg chol, 534 mg sod**

Grilled Southwestern Pasta Salad

STEAK • MULTIGRAIN PASTA • SERVES 4 • TOTAL: 40 MIN • SERVE AT ROOM TEMPERATURE

✳

8 oz multigrain or whole-wheat penne pasta

8 oz lean boneless sirloin steak

½ tsp *each* ground cumin, salt and pepper

3 medium poblano chile peppers, halved and seeded

1 ear fresh corn, husked

1 medium sweet onion, sliced ½-in. thick

Cooking spray

2 large ripe tomatoes, cut in bite-size chunks

1 Tbsp olive oil

¼ cup lime juice

½ cup chopped cilantro

1. Cook pasta in a large pot of lightly salted boiling water as package directs. Drain; rinse under cold water and drain again. Transfer to a large serving bowl.

2. Heat outdoor grill. Rub steak with ¼ tsp each of the cumin, salt and pepper. Coat steak, peppers, corn and onion with cooking spray.

3. Grill steak 4 to 6 minutes, turning once, for medium-rare. Remove to cutting board; let stand 5 minutes. Grill peppers, corn and onion 8 to 10 minutes, turning as needed until lightly charred and tender.

4. Cut peppers and onion into bite-size pieces and cut corn off cob; add to bowl with pasta. Slice steak thinly against the grain and add to bowl.

5. Add remaining cumin, salt and pepper and remaining ingredients to bowl; toss to mix and coat.

PER SERVING: 410 cal, 25 g pro, 65 g car, 8 g fiber, 9 g fat (2 g sat fat), 38 mg chol, 331 mg sod

Spaghetti all' Amatriciana

BACON • SERVES 4 • TOTAL TIME: 20 MIN

❊

4 strips (about 4 oz) bacon or pancetta (Italian bacon), cut in ¼-in. pieces

1 Tbsp olive oil

1 cup finely chopped onion

½ tsp crushed red pepper flakes

1 lb spaghetti, linguine, bucatini or tubular pasta such as macaroni or ziti

1 can (28 oz) Italian plum tomatoes, well drained in a colander

½ tsp salt

⅓ cup grated Parmesan or Romano cheese, plus extra to serve at the table

1. Bring a large pot of lightly salted water to a boil.

2. Meanwhile, heat bacon and oil in a large nonstick skillet over medium heat, separating bacon pieces with a wooden spoon. Sauté 3 minutes until almost crisp.

3. Add onion and red pepper flakes. Cook, stirring, 5 minutes or until onion is soft.

4. Stir pasta into boiling water and cook as package directs, stirring occasionally.

5. Add tomatoes to skillet and break up with the side of wooden spoon. Reduce heat, add salt and simmer 8 minutes or until sauce is thick and chunky.

6. Drain pasta and place in a large serving bowl. Add sauce; toss to mix. Add ⅓ cup cheese and toss again. Serve immediately; pass extra cheese at the table.

PER SERVING: **691 cal, 22 g pro, 97 g car, 5 g fiber, 24 g fat (8 g sat fat), 24 mg chol, 1,316 mg sod**

Penne with Bacon, Spinach & Mushrooms

BACON • SERVES 6 • TOTAL TIME: 30 MIN

1 box (16 oz) penne pasta

10 slices bacon (about ½ lb)

1 medium onion, halved and sliced thin

1 pkg (8 oz) sliced mushrooms

2 cloves garlic, sliced

¼ tsp crushed red pepper flakes

1 pkg (12 oz) fresh baby spinach

GARNISH: grated Parmesan cheese

1. Cook pasta in a large pot of lightly salted boiling water as package directs.

2. Meanwhile, cook bacon in a large, deep nonstick skillet over medium heat until browned. Remove bacon to paper towels to drain. Remove all but 2 Tbsp fat from skillet.

3. Add onion and mushrooms to skillet; sauté 5 minutes until onion is golden. Add garlic and red pepper flakes; cook 30 seconds until fragrant. Add spinach; cover and cook, stirring occasionally, 2 minutes until wilted.

4. Drain pasta, reserving 1 cup pasta water. Add pasta to skillet with some of the reserved pasta water; toss. Add more water as necessary. Crumble bacon on top of pasta and serve with Parmesan cheese.

PER SERVING: 406 cal, 16 g pro, 61 g car, 8 g fiber, 11 g fat (4 g sat fat), 13 mg chol, 340 mg sod

White Beans, Sausage & Arugula Pasta

PORK SAUSAGE • SERVES 4 • TOTAL TIME: 15 MIN

✳

12 oz spaghettini pasta

12 oz hot or sweet Italian sausage, casing removed

1 medium onion, quartered, thinly sliced

1 can (14 oz) roasted garlic-flavored chicken broth

1 can (19 oz) cannellini beans, rinsed

1 bag (4 oz) baby arugula or 1 bag (5 oz) baby spinach, washed

GARNISH: grated Parmesan cheese

1. Cook pasta in a large pot of lightly salted boiling water as package directs. Drain; return to pot.

2. Meanwhile, heat a large nonstick skillet over medium-high heat. Add sausage and onion and, breaking up sausage with a wooden spoon, sauté 6 minutes or until no longer pink. Add broth and beans; bring to a boil. Reduce heat; simmer 3 minutes to blend flavors.

3. Pour over pasta, add arugula and toss to mix and coat. Top with Parmesan cheese.

PER SERVING: 748 cal, 31 g pro, 89 g car, 10 g fiber, 29 g fat (10 g sat), 66 mg chol, 1,256 mg sod

Ham & Cheese Lasagna

HAM · SERVES 8 · TOTAL TIME: ABOUT 1 HR 30 MIN

CHEESE SAUCE

2 cans (10.75 oz each) condensed Cheddar cheese soup

1¼ cups lowfat milk

1 can (14.5 oz) no-salt-added diced tomatoes, drained, large pieces cut up

1 Tbsp *each* dry mustard and instant minced onion

½ cup shredded Cheddar cheese

¼ cup grated Parmesan cheese

1 tub (15 oz) ricotta cheese

2 large eggs

¼ cup grated Parmesan cheese

¾ tsp ground nutmeg

12 uncooked, flat oven-ready lasagna noodles

1 bag (16 oz) frozen chopped broccoli, thawed, pressed dry on paper towels

1½ cups shredded Cheddar cheese

8 oz thinly sliced baked Virginia ham

1 jar (12 oz) roasted red peppers, well drained and chopped

1. Preheat oven to 375°F. Lightly coat a 13 x 9-in. baking dish with cooking spray.

2. CHEESE SAUCE: Whisk all sauce ingredients in a 2-qt saucepan until blended. Heat, stirring with a whisk, until cheeses melt.

3. Mix ricotta, eggs, Parmesan cheese and nutmeg in a bowl until thoroughly combined.

4. Layer lasagna in prepared baking dish as follows: spread 1 cup cheese sauce over bottom, top with 4 overlapping noodles, ½ the ricotta mixture, the broccoli, 1½ cups cheese sauce and ½ cup Cheddar cheese.

5. Add 4 more noodles, the remaining ricotta mixture, the ham, ½ cup Cheddar cheese, the chopped peppers and 1½ cups cheese sauce.

6. Finish with rest of noodles, cheese sauce and Cheddar cheese. Cover tightly with foil.

7. Bake 50 minutes or until sauce bubbles and noodles are tender. Uncover; bake 10 minutes longer. Let stand 15 minutes before cutting and serving.

PER SERVING: 543 cal, 34 g pro, 41 g car, 3 g fiber, 28 g fat (15 g sat fat), 148 mg chol, 1,864 mg sod

Linguine with Pork & Vegetables

PORK CHOPS · SERVES 4 · TOTAL TIME: ABOUT 25 MIN

❋

8 oz linguine pasta

1 lb thinly sliced boneless pork chops

1 red bell pepper

⅛ tsp *each* salt and pepper

1 bag (9 oz) microwavable leafy greens blend (a mix of tender baby spinach and other fresh vegetables) or baby spinach

¾ cup bottled citrus stir-fry sauce or regular stir-fry sauce

1. Bring a large pot of lightly salted water to a boil. Add linguine and cook as package directs.

2. Meanwhile, cut pork chops and red bell pepper into narrow strips. Season pork with the salt and pepper.

3. Coat a large nonstick skillet with cooking spray. Heat over medium-high heat, add ½ the pork and stir-fry 1 to 2 minutes just until cooked through. Remove to a plate. Respray skillet; stir-fry remaining pork; add to plate.

4. Wash skillet; coat with cooking spray. Heat over medium-high heat, add pepper strips and stir-fry 2 minutes or until tinged brown and crisp-tender. Add greens, a few handfuls at a time, adding more as they cook down. Cook until wilted.

5. Drain linguine, transfer to a large bowl and add pork, vegetables and stir-fry sauce; toss to mix and coat.

PER SERVING: **487 cal, 32 g pro, 54 g car, 3 g fiber, 16 g fat (5 g sat fat), 76 mg chol, 1,194 mg sod**

Pasta with Shrimp & Eggplant

SHRIMP • WHOLE-WHEAT PASTA • SERVES 4 • TOTAL TIME: 25 MIN

2 tsp olive oil

1½ lb eggplant, cut in ¾-in. cubes

8 oz low-carb or whole-wheat spaghetti pasta

1 *each* red and yellow bell pepper, cut in thin strips

1 medium red onion, thinly sliced

1 tsp dried oregano

1 lb raw large shrimp, peeled and deveined

10 pitted Kalamata olives, halved

¾ cup (3 oz) crumbled feta cheese

GARNISH: chopped parsley

1. Bring a large pot of lightly salted water to a boil.

2. Heat oil in a large nonstick skillet over medium-high heat. Add eggplant; sauté 6 minutes or until almost soft.

3. Stir pasta into boiling water. Cook as package directs. Ladle off ½ cup cooking water; reserve. Drain pasta, return to pot and add reserved water.

4. Meanwhile, add pepper strips, onion and oregano to eggplant. Sauté 6 minutes until crisp-tender. Stir in shrimp, cover and steam, stirring once, 2 to 4 minutes, until shrimp are just done. Add to pasta in pot. Toss to mix and coat. Pour into a serving bowl. Add olives and cheese. Sprinkle with parsley. Toss again just before serving.

PER SERVING: **474 cal, 32 g pro, 63 g car, 8 g fiber, 13 g fat (4 g sat fat), 159 mg chol, 998 mg sod**

Pad Thai

SHRIMP • SERVES 4 • TOTAL TIME: ABOUT 55 MIN

8 oz ⅛-in.-wide flat rice sticks

¼ cup *each* bottled fish sauce and seasoned rice vinegar

2 Tbsp fresh lime juice

1 Tbsp sugar

3 Tbsp peanut oil

1 lb raw shrimp (any size), peeled and deveined

1 Tbsp minced garlic

2 large eggs

8 thinly sliced radishes

4 scallions, cut in 1-in. lengths

¼ cup dry-roasted unsalted peanuts, finely chopped

¼ cup packed cilantro leaves, finely chopped

1. Soak rice sticks in warm water to cover 20 minutes until softened (see FYI).

2. Meanwhile, mix fish sauce, vinegar, lime juice and sugar in a cup.

3. Heat 1 Tbsp oil in a large nonstick skillet over medium-high heat. Add shrimp and garlic; sauté 1 to 3 minutes until cooked through. Transfer to a plate.

4. Heat remaining 2 Tbsp oil over medium-high heat. Add eggs; stir just until set. Add radishes, scallions, drained rice sticks and fish-sauce mixture. Cook, stirring, 1 minute or until rice sticks soften and wilt.

5. Place on a serving platter; top with shrimp, peanuts and cilantro. Toss to mix.

PER SERVING: **568 cal, 31 g pro, 63 g car, 1 g fiber, 21 g fat (4 g sat fat), 279 mg chol, 1,198 mg sod**

FYI The rice sticks will still be a bit stiff after soaking but will soften while cooking.

Seaside Mac'N'Cheese

SHRIMP • SERVES 4 • TOTAL TIME: 12 MIN

✳

2 boxes (12 oz each) creamy cheese-sauce-and-shell pasta

1 bag (12 oz) frozen medium shrimp, cooked, peeled and deveined

1 cup bottled salsa

GARNISH: chopped cilantro

1. Cook pasta shells in a large pot of lightly salted boiling water as package directs. Two minutes before pasta is done, add frozen shrimp. Cook, stirring often, 2 minutes or until shrimp are hot.

2. Drain pasta and shrimp in a colander; return to pot. Stir in cheese sauce from packets. Pour into serving dish. Top servings with salsa. Serve with a green salad.

PER SERVING: 646 cal, 39 g pro, 72 g car, 3 g fiber, 20 g fat (8 g sat fat), 203 mg chol, 2,146 mg sod

PERFECT PASTA

- For each pound of pasta, bring 4 to 6 quarts of water to a rapid boil. (A covered pot will boil sooner.)
- Add 2 teaspoons salt, then stir in pasta. Adjust heat so water keeps boiling briskly and pasta keeps moving.
- Cook uncovered, stirring often for the first 2 to 3 minutes, then stirring every few minutes.
- Set a timer for cooking time stated on pasta package. Check doneness toward end by biting into a piece or strand; it should still be slightly firm at center.
- If a recipe calls for adding pasta cooking water to the sauce (it makes the sauce a bit more saucy), use a ladle to scoop water.
- Drain pasta into a colander set in a sink with an open drain. To help empty pasta shapes that may catch water, shake the colander a few times. Immediately return pasta to pot, add sauce and toss to mix and coat.

Shrimp & Linguine Alfredo

SHRIMP • SERVES 6 • TOTAL TIME: 25 MIN

ALFREDO SAUCE

3 Tbsp olive oil spread

3 Tbsp flour

2 cups fat-free half-and-half

½ tsp *each* salt and freshly ground pepper

¼ tsp ground nutmeg

¾ cup grated Parmesan cheese

1 lb linguine pasta

1 bag (9 to 10 oz) baby spinach

1 bag (12 oz) frozen peeled and deveined raw extra-large shrimp, thawed

1 Tbsp minced garlic

1 pt (12 oz) grape tomatoes

1. Bring a large pot of lightly salted water to a boil.

2. Meanwhile, make Alfredo sauce: Melt olive oil spread in a 2-qt saucepan over medium heat. Whisk in flour to blend. Add half-and-half, salt, pepper and nutmeg. Cook, whisking constantly, 5 minutes or until simmering and slightly thickened. Remove from heat; whisk in cheese until well blended. Cover to keep warm.

3. Stir pasta into the boiling water. Cook as package directs, adding spinach 1 minute before pasta is done.

4. While pasta cooks, put 2 Tbsp water, the shrimp and garlic in a large nonstick skillet. Sauté over medium-high heat 2 to 3 minutes. Add tomatoes; sauté 2 minutes or until tomatoes just begin to split and shrimp are opaque at centers. Remove from heat.

5. Drain pasta and spinach and return to pot. Add sauce, shrimp and tomatoes. Toss to mix and coat.

PER SERVING: 521 cal, 27 g pro, 76 g car, 5 g fiber, 9 g fat (3 g sat fat), 94 mg chol, 942 mg sod

Pasta Primavera with Shrimp & Basil

SHRIMP • SERVES 4 • TOTAL TIME: ABOUT 35 MIN

12 oz linguine pasta

1 cup fresh small broccoli florets 4 Tbsp olive oil

12 oz raw medium shrimp, peeled and deveined

1 *each* small red, yellow and orange bell pepper, quartered lengthwise, cut crosswise in narrow strips

1 cup (4 oz) haricot vert (thin French-style green beans) or regular green beans, stem ends trimmed, cut in half crosswise

5 medium (4 oz) fresh asparagus, woody ends snapped off, spears cut in 1-in. pieces

1¼ cups (4 oz) fresh sugar snap peas, stem ends trimmed

2 tsp minced garlic

¾ tsp *each* salt and freshly ground pepper

1 pt (12 oz) grape tomatoes, cut in half

2 cups fresh basil leaves, stacked, rolled up, then cut crosswise in narrow strips

⅓ cup grated Parmesan cheese

2 tsp freshly grated lemon peel

GARNISH: additional cheese, if desired

1. Bring a large pot of lightly salted water to a boil. Add pasta and cook as package directs, adding broccoli about 1 minute before pasta is done. Remove and reserve ¾ cup cooking water; drain pasta and broccoli well in a colander.

2. Meanwhile, heat 1 Tbsp oil in a deep 12-in. nonstick skillet over medium heat. Add shrimp and sauté 2 to 3 minutes or until just cooked through. Transfer to a plate.

3. Heat remaining 3 Tbsp oil in skillet. Add the peppers, beans, asparagus, peas, garlic, salt and pepper. Sauté 4 to 5 minutes until vegetables are crisp-tender. Stir in reserved cooking water, the tomatoes and shrimp and cook 1 minute or until heated through.

4. Return pasta and broccoli to pot, then add mixture in skillet and the remaining ingredients; toss to mix and coat. Serve immediately.

PER SERVING: 599 cal, 32 g pro, 77 g car, 7 g fiber, 18 g fat (4 g sat fat), 110 mg chol, 980 mg sod

Linguine with Shrimp Arrabbiata

SHRIMP • SERVES 4 • TOTAL TIME: 21 MIN

12 oz linguine pasta

1½ tsp olive oil

1 lb large raw shrimp (26 to 30), thawed if frozen, peeled and deveined

¼ cup dry white wine (optional)

1 tub (15 oz) refrigerated arrabbiata sauce

⅓ cup chopped parsley

1. Cook pasta in a large pot of lightly salted boiling water as package directs.

2. Meanwhile, heat oil in a large nonstick skillet. Add shrimp; sauté over high heat 1 minute or just until shrimp turn pink.

3. Add wine, if using; cook a few seconds until most evaporates. Add sauce; heat just until simmering and shrimp are cooked through.

4. Drain pasta; return to pot. Add sauce and parsley; toss to mix.

PER SERVING: 503 cal, 35 g pro, 72 g car, 4 g fiber, 10 g fat (2 g sat fat), 173 mg chol, 985 mg sod

HINT Delicious with warm garlic bread and green salad.

Fettuccine with Tuna-Scallion Sauce

TUNA • SERVES 4 • TOTAL TIME: 15 MIN

❀

8 oz green beans, trimmed and cut in 2-in. lengths

12 oz fettuccine pasta

2 cans (6 oz each) solid white tuna, packed in oil

2 cups sliced scallions

2 lemons, peel and 3 Tbsp juice

1. Bring a large pot of lightly salted water to a boil. Add beans to boiling pasta water at same time as pasta.

2. Drain oil from 1 can tuna into a medium nonstick skillet (discard oil from other can).

3. Add scallions to skillet and sauté over medium heat 2 minutes. Cover skillet; remove from heat.

4. Grate peel from lemons. Squeeze 3 Tbsp juice.

5. Ladle out and reserve ⅓ cup cooking water from pasta and beans, then drain.

6. Toss pasta and beans with tuna, breaking up tuna. Add scallions, lemon peel and juice, along with reserved cooking water. Toss and serve.

PER SERVING: 515 cal, 34 g pro, 72 g car, 4 g fiber, 10 g fat (1 g sat fat), 29 mg chol, 412 mg sod

ADDED TOUCH: Toss pasta and sauce with ½ cup crumbled feta cheese just before serving.

Pasta with Tuna, Green Beans, Potatoes & Almonds

TUNA • SERVES 6 • TOTAL TIME: 40 MIN

⅓ cup whole natural almonds (with skins)

3 medium red potatoes, scrubbed, cut in ¾-in. pieces

8 oz fresh green beans, trimmed, cut in 1-in. lengths

1 lb linguine pasta

1 can (6 oz) light tuna in olive oil, oil drained and reserved, tuna flaked

1 Tbsp minced garlic

1. Bring a large pot of lightly salted water to a boil.

2. Meanwhile, toast almonds in a large nonstick skillet over medium heat, stirring often, 5 minutes or until fragrant. Let cool, then coarsely chop.

3. Put potatoes in skillet with water to cover by ½ in. Bring to a boil, add beans and boil gently 5 minutes or until potatoes and beans are tender. Drain well; wipe skillet dry.

4. Meanwhile, add pasta to the boiling water and cook as package directs.

5. Heat oil reserved from tuna in dried skillet over medium heat. Add potatoes and beans, and sauté 5 minutes or until potatoes are golden. Add garlic and stir 1 to 2 minutes until fragrant. Stir in tuna.

6. Ladle off 1 cup cooking water from pasta; stir into skillet mixture. Drain pasta and put into a warmed large serving bowl. Add tuna mixture and toss to mix well. Sprinkle with toasted almonds.

PER SERVING: 448 cal, 19 g pro, 76 g car, 5 g fiber, 7 g fat (1 g sat fat), 10 mg chol, 145 mg sod

Sicilian Pasta with Tuna

TUNA • SERVES 4 • TOTAL TIME: 22 MIN

12 oz spaghetti pasta

2 tsp olive oil

1 large onion, sliced

1 jar (8.5 oz) olive spread or
1 can (7.5 oz) eggplant appetizer
(caponata) plus ¼ cup chopped
pimiento-stuffed olives

1 can (6 oz) chunk light tuna
in olive oil, drained

1 Tbsp raisins

¼ tsp pepper

GARNISH: chopped parsley

1. Bring a large pot of lightly salted water to a boil. Add pasta and cook as package directs.

2. Meanwhile, heat oil in a large nonstick skillet over medium-high heat. Add onion and sauté 7 minutes until golden and tender. Reduce heat to medium, add remaining ingredients and stir gently until heated through.

3. Remove ½ cup pasta cooking water. Drain pasta; return to pot. Add olive mixture and reserved pasta water; toss to mix and coat. Sprinkle with chopped parsley.

PER SERVING: **542 cal, 20 g pro, 76 g car, 3 g fiber, 17 g fat (2 g sat fat), 15 mg chol, 945 mg sod**

Linguine with Clams & Parsley

CLAMS • SERVES 4 • TOTAL TIME: 15 MIN

12 oz linguine pasta

½ cup dry white wine (or chicken broth)

1 small onion, finely chopped

2 Tbsp minced garlic

2 cans (6.5 oz each) chopped clams, drained, juice reserved

1 cup chicken broth

¾ cup chopped fresh parsley

2 tsp freshly grated lemon zest

Juice from 1 medium lemon

½ tsp salt

⅛ tsp freshly ground pepper

1. Cook pasta in a large pot of lightly salted boiling water as package directs.

2. While pasta cooks, put wine (or chicken broth), onion and garlic in a large saucepan over medium heat and bring to a simmer. Cover and cook 5 minutes or until onion is soft.

3. Add reserved clam juice and 1 cup chicken broth. Bring to a simmer and cook uncovered 3 to 5 minutes for flavors to blend. Stir in clams; heat through.

4. Drain pasta; return to pot. Add clam sauce and remaining ingredients; toss to mix and coat.

PER SERVING: 439 cal, 25 g pro, 72 g car, 3 g fiber, 3 g fat (0 g sat fat), 32 mg chol, 607 mg sod

Spaghetti with Mussels & White Wine

MUSSELS • SERVES 4 • TOTAL TIME: ABOUT 20 MIN

12 oz spaghetti pasta

1 Tbsp olive oil

2 tsp chopped garlic

2 lb scrubbed mussels (discard any open mussels)

½ cup dry white wine

1 Tbsp grated lemon zest

2 Tbsp capers

½ tsp salt

¼ tsp crushed red pepper flakes

3 Tbsp snipped chives or sliced scallions or chopped parsley

1. Cook pasta in a large pot of lightly salted boiling water as package directs, reserving 1 cup cooking water before draining.

2. Meanwhile, heat olive oil in large nonstick skillet over medium heat. Add chopped garlic; cook 30 seconds until fragrant. Add scrubbed mussels, white wine, grated lemon zest, capers, salt and red pepper flakes. Cover and cook 3 to 5 minutes until mussel shells open.

3. Toss with drained pasta, chives (or scallions or parsley), and reserved cooking water as needed.

PER SERVING: 420 cal, 20 g pro, 68 g car, 2 g fiber, 6 g fat (1 g sat fat), 21 mg chol, 639 mg sod

Lemony Salmon Fettuccine

SALMON FILLET • SERVES 6 • TOTAL TIME: 28 MIN

1 lb fettuccine pasta

2 cups frozen petite green peas

1 jar (16 oz) Alfredo sauce

1 piece (8 oz) fresh salmon fillet, sliced from skin in thin 2 x 1-in. pieces

⅓ cup finely chopped fresh dill

1 Tbsp freshly grated lemon zest

4 thin lemon wedges (optional)

1. Bring a large pot of lightly salted water to a boil. Add pasta and cook 7 minutes, stirring often. Add peas; boil 5 to 6 minutes until pasta is firm-tender and peas are done.

2. Meanwhile, stir Alfredo sauce in a medium saucepan over medium-low heat 3 minutes, or until simmering. Add salmon and, stirring gently with a rubber spatula, simmer 1 to 2 minutes until fish is opaque. Cover; remove from heat.

3. Remove ½ cup cooking water from pot. Drain pasta and peas; return to pot. Add sauce, reserved cooking water, dill and lemon zest. Gently turn with a rubber spatula to mix and coat.

4. Serve with lemon wedges to squeeze over pasta.

PER SERVING: 511 cal, 21 g pro, 66 g car, 4 g fiber, 13 g fat (6 g sat fat), 73 mg chol, 906 mg sod

Fettuccine with Smoked Salmon

SMOKED SALMON • SERVES 6 • TOTAL TIME: ABOUT 20 MIN

12 oz fettuccine pasta

4 oz smoked salmon

1 tub (6.5 oz) cucumber-dill spreadable cheese

⅓ cup *each* sliced scallions and snipped dill

1 Tbsp cappers

¼ tsp pepper

1. Cook pasta in a large pot of lightly salted boiling water as package directs, reserving ½ cup cooking water before draining.

2. Meanwhile, cut smoked salmon in strips.

3. In a large bowl combine salmon with cucumber-dill spreadable cheese, sliced scallions and snipped dill, capers and pepper.

4. Add pasta and reserved water; toss to mix.

PER SERVING: 307 cal, 15 g pro, 47 g car, 3 g fiber, 7 g fat (4 g sat fat), 24 mg chol, 277 mg sod

Pasta with Salmon & Spinach

SALMON FILLET • SERVES 4 • TOTAL TIME: 21 MIN

1 bag (10 oz) prewashed spinach, tough stems removed, leaves coarsely chopped

1 box (12 oz) mafalda (mini lasagna) or broad egg noodles

2 tsp olive oil

2 Tbsp minced garlic

1 can (14.5 oz) diced tomatoes

1 can (14.5 oz) chicken broth

2 lemons

1 lb fresh salmon fillet, skin and bones removed (see Tip), fish cut in paper-thin slivers

GARNISH: shaved Parmesan cheese

1. Set a colander in kitchen sink and put spinach in colander.

2. Cook pasta in a large pot of lightly salted boiling water as package directs.

3. Meanwhile, heat oil in a large skillet over medium-high heat until hot, but not smoking. Add garlic and sauté 1 minute. Add tomatoes and broth. Bring to a boil, reduce heat, cover and simmer 5 minutes for flavors to blend.

4. As pasta and sauce cook, grate peel from lemons and squeeze out 3 Tbsp juice.

5. Drain pasta in colander with the spinach. Return pasta and spinach to pot, add broth mixture and toss to mix and coat. Add salmon and lemon peel and juice; toss again.

6. Serve immediately. Top with the Parmesan cheese.

PER SERVING: **599 cal, 37 g pro, 73 g car, 4 g fiber, 17 g fat (3 g saturated fat), 67 mg chol, 710 mg sod**

TIP Fillet usually refers to a boneless piece of fish, but double-check for bones by running your fingers over the fillet. If you feel bones, pull them out with your fingers or tweezers.

Penne with Caesar Sauce

ANCHOVY FILLETS • SERVES 6 • TOTAL TIME: 8 MIN

1 lb penne rigate pasta

SAUCE

1 tub (15 oz) part-skim ricotta
cheese

1 can (2 oz) flat anchovy fillets,
drained

2 Tbsp fresh lemon juice

1½ tsp bottled chopped garlic in oil

1⅓ cup grated Parmesan cheese

2 bags (6 oz each) prewashed baby
spinach

3 Tbsp grated Parmesan cheese

1. Cook pasta in a large pot of lightly salted boiling water as
package directs.

2. Meanwhile, purée Sauce ingredients in a food processor
until smooth. With processor running, gradually add ⅓ cup
of the pasta cooking water.

3. Put spinach in colander in sink. Drain pasta over spinach.
Transfer spinach and pasta to pot and add sauce. Toss to mix.
Sprinkle with Parmesan cheese.

PER SERVING: 458 cal, 24 g pro, 68 g car, 5 g fiber,
10 g fat (5 g sat fat), 32 mg chol, 863 mg sod

Linguine & Garlic Oil

VEGETARIAN • SERVES 6 • TOTAL TIME: 35 MIN

1 lb linguine pasta

SAUCE

⅓ cup extra-virgin olive oil

3 large cloves garlic, finely chopped

½ tsp salt

¼ tsp crushed red pepper flakes

¼ cup finely chopped Italian parsley

1½ Tbsp butter, softened

1 tsp finely grated lemon peel

1. Cook pasta in a large pot of lightly salted boiling water as package directs.

2. Meanwhile, heat olive oil, garlic, salt and red pepper flakes in a covered pan over very low heat just until garlic is soft.

3. Remove and reserve ¾ cup pasta cooking water. Drain pasta; transfer to serving bowl. Toss with oil mixture, the water, parsley, butter and lemon peel.

PER SERVING: 416 cal, 10 g pro, 58 g car, 2 g fiber, 16 g fat (4 g sat fat), 8 mg chol, 487 mg sod

Linguine With No-Cook Tomato Sauce

SERVES 8 • TOTAL TIME: ABOUT 21 MIN • SERVE AT ROOM TEMPERATURE

SAUCE

3 cups chopped ripe tomatoes

4 oz mozzarella cheese, cut in ½-in. cubes

⅓ cup fresh basil leaves, chopped

¼ cup olive oil

½ tsp *each* minced garlic and salt

¼ tsp pepper

1 lb linguine pasta

1. Bring a large pot of lightly salted water to a boil.

2. Meanwhile, put all the Sauce ingredients in a large serving bowl. Toss gently to mix and coat.

3. Cook linguine as package directs. Drain well; add to sauce and toss to mix.

PER SERVING: 326 cal, 11 g pro, 46 g car, 2 g fiber, 11 g fat (3 g sat fat), 11 mg chol, 208 mg sod

TIP Make the sauce before cooking the pasta so the flavors have a chance to blend. Spinach salad goes well with this.

Macaroni & Cheese

SERVES 6 • TOTAL TIME: 20 MIN

1 lb cavatappi or other short pasta

2½ cups milk

3 Tbsp flour

½ tsp *each* salt, onion powder and paprika

1 Tbsp Dijon mustard

1 bag (8 oz) Classic Melts 4-cheese blend

1 cup fresh bread crumbs

2 Tbsp grated Parmesan cheese

GARNISH: sliced scallions and paprika

1. Cook pasta in a large pot of lightly salted boiling water as package directs. If making crumb-topped version, grease a shallow 2-qt baking dish.

2. While pasta cooks, whisk milk, flour, salt, onion powder and paprika in a medium saucepan until blended. Bring to a boil over medium-high heat, whisking often. Reduce heat and simmer 2 minutes until slightly thickened.

3. Over low heat, whisk in mustard, then cheese blend until melted and smooth.

4. Drain pasta; return to pot, add sauce and toss to coat. Garnish with scallions and a sprinkling of paprika and serve immediately. If making crumb-topped version, transfer to the prepared baking dish, sprinkle with bread crumbs and Parmesan cheese and broil 2 to 3 minutes until crumbs are toasted.

PER SERVING: **524 cal, 21 g pro, 71 g car, 2 g fiber, 16 g fat (9 g sat fat), 56 mg chol, 886 mg sod**

FYI This recipe features two ways to enjoy the family favorite: creamy or crumb-topped.

Farfalle with Pesto, Goat Cheese & Grape Tomatoes

SERVES 6 • TOTAL TIME: 25 MIN

1 lb farfalle (bow-tie) pasta

SAUCE

¼ cup *each* chopped walnuts and extra-virgin olive oil

2 cups fresh basil leaves

2 small cloves garlic, smashed

½ tsp *each* crushed red pepper flakes and salt

4 oz goat cheese, crumbled

1 pt (12 oz) grape or cherry tomatoes, cut in half

1. Cook pasta in a large pot of lightly salted boiling water as package directs.

2. Meanwhile, put walnuts, oil, basil, garlic, crushed pepper and salt in a blender; blend until puréed.

3. Remove and reserve ¼ cup pasta cooking water. Drain pasta; transfer to serving bowl. Add ½ of the goat cheese and tomatoes. Toss to mix. Add basil mixture and reserved cooking water; toss to coat. Spoon remaining goat cheese over top.

PER SERVING: 477 cal, 16 g pro, 61 g car, 4 g fiber, 20 g fat (6 g sat fat), 15 mg chol, 559 mg sod

Fettuccine with Cheese Sauce

SERVES 4 • TOTAL TIME: ABOUT 27 MIN

12 oz fettuccine pasta

2 cups frozen green peas

2 tsp minced garlic

5 cups (5 oz) coarsely chopped fresh spinach leaves

1¼ cups bottled Alfredo sauce

⅓ cup 1% lowfat milk

1 pt (12 oz) cherry or grape tomatoes, cut in half

1. Cook pasta in a large pot of lightly salted boiling water as package directs. Put frozen peas in a colander set in sink.

2. While pasta cooks, coat a large skillet with cooking spray. Heat over medium-low heat; add garlic and cook 1 minute or until soft. Stir in spinach; cook until wilted. Stir in Alfredo sauce and milk. Cook 1 or 2 minutes to heat.

3. Drain pasta over peas in colander (see Tip). Transfer to a large serving bowl and add sauce and tomatoes; toss to mix and coat.

PER SERVING: **525 cal, 19 g pro, 81 g car, 6 g fiber, 13 g fat (8 g sat fat), 51 mg chol, 617 mg sod**

TIP Draining the pasta in the colander with the frozen peas thaws and heats the peas without the need for further cooking.

Penne Greek-Style with Chickpeas

SERVES 4 • TOTAL TIME: 22 MIN

12 oz penne rigate pasta

1 can (15 oz) chickpeas, drained

1 jar (7 oz) roasted peppers, drained and sliced

1 jar (6 oz) quartered marinated artichoke hearts, undrained

½ cup sliced scallions

¼ cup Kalamata olives, pitted

1 cup crumbled feta cheese

1. Cook pasta in a large pot of lightly salted boiling water as package directs, reserving 1 cup cooking water before draining.

2. Meanwhile, in a large nonstick skillet over medium-high heat, toss chickpeas, roasted peppers, marinated artichoke hearts, sliced scallions and pitted Kalamata olives until hot.

3. Toss with drained pasta, crumbled feta cheese, pepper to taste and reserved cooking water as needed.

PER SERVING: **633 cal, 22 g pro, 95 g car, 8 g fiber, 18 g fat (8 g sat fat), 34 mg chol, 962 mg sod**

Tortellini with Creamy Butternut Squash

SERVES 4 • TOTAL TIME: ABOUT 25 MIN

1 cup milk

3 cups fresh butternut squash, peeled and cut in ½-in. pieces

1 red bell pepper, coarsely chopped

1 Tbsp chopped fresh sage (or 1½ tsp dried)

2 pkg (9 oz each) refrigerated cheese tortellini

1 pkg (5.2 oz) garlic & herb cheese spread

1. Heat milk, butternut squash, pepper and sage in a medium saucepan over medium heat until simmering. Cover and cook 8 minutes or until squash is tender.

2. Meanwhile, boil cheese tortellini in a large pot of lightly salted boiling water as package directs, reserving 1 cup cooking water before draining.

3. Remove saucepan from heat; stir in garlic & herb cheese spread. Toss with drained tortellini and reserved cooking water as needed.

PER SERVING: **640 cal, 24 g pro, 78 g car, 6 g fiber, 28 g fat (15 g sat fat), 99 mg chol, 834 mg sod**

Gnocchi with Broccolini & Mushrooms

SERVES 4 • TOTAL TIME: 35 MIN

3 Tbsp olive oil

12 oz assorted mushrooms (see Tip) or white mushrooms, sliced

1 tsp salt

1 Tbsp minced garlic

1 cup fat-free chicken broth

2 bunches broccolini (about 1 lb), ends trimmed, halved crosswise

¼ tsp crushed red pepper flakes

1 bag (16 oz) frozen potato gnocchi

GARNISH: shredded Parmesan cheese

1. Bring a large pot of lightly salted water to a boil.

2. Heat 1 Tbsp oil in a large nonstick skillet over medium heat. Add mushrooms and, stirring occasionally, cook 4 to 5 minutes until tender (mushrooms will release their liquid). Increase heat to medium-high, add salt and cook 4 to 5 minutes until liquid evaporates and mushrooms are golden brown. Remove to serving bowl. Reduce heat to medium.

3. Heat remaining 2 Tbsp oil and garlic in skillet about 1 minute until garlic is fragrant. Add broth, broccolini and red pepper flakes, cover and simmer 8 to 10 minutes until stems are tender.

4. Meanwhile, add gnocchi to pot; cover just until water returns to a boil. Uncover; cook as package directs. Drain; add to serving bowl along with broccolini; toss to mix. Sprinkle servings with Parmesan cheese.

PER SERVING: 431 cal, 17 g pro, 66 g car, 6 g fiber, 12 g fat (2 g sat fat), 17 mg chol, 1,544 mg sod

TIP If including shiitakes, discard stems.

Gnocchi Primavera

SERVES 4 • TOTAL TIME: ABOUT 26 MIN

1 bunch (about 1 lb) asparagus, woody ends snapped off, spears cut crosswise in thirds

2 medium yellow summer squash, cut in ½ lengthwise, then crosswise in ½-in. pieces

1 bag (16 oz) frozen gnocchi

¾ cup basil pesto (see Note)

½ cup reduced-fat sour cream

1 pt (12 oz) grape tomatoes, cut in half

GARNISH: grated Parmesan cheese

1. Bring a large pot of lightly salted water to a boil.

2. Add asparagus and squash to pot; return to a boil and boil 1 minute. Add gnocchi; cover pot just until water returns to a boil. Uncover and cook 2 minutes more or until gnocchi float to surface and vegetables are crisp-tender. Drain in a colander; transfer to a serving bowl.

3. Mix pesto and sour cream in pot. Stir in tomatoes. Pour over gnocchi; toss gently to mix and coat. Serve with Parmesan cheese, if desired.

PER SERVING: **506 cal, 15 g pro, 55 g car, 6 g fiber, 27 g fat (6 g sat fat), 17 mg chol, 834 mg sod**

NOTE Look for tubs of pesto in your market's fresh pasta or dairy section.

Fettuccine with Cilantro Pesto Sauce

SERVES 6 • TOTAL TIME: 10 MIN

1 lb fettuccine pasta

PESTO

2 cups *each* fresh cilantro and parsley

1 can (4 oz) green chilies, drained

⅓ cup unsalted roasted peanuts

¼ cup fresh lime juice

2 Tbsp olive oil

1 Tbsp bottled chopped garlic in oil

½ tsp *each* ground cumin and salt

1 can (about 16 oz) black beans, rinsed (see Tip)

1 can (11 oz) Mexican-style corn, drained

1. Cook pasta in a large pot of lightly salted boiling water as package directs. Remove and reserve ⅓ cup pasta cooking water.

2. Meanwhile, purée Pesto ingredients in food processor until smooth. With processor running, gradually add reserved pasta cooking water.

3. Drain pasta, return to pot and add pesto and remaining ingredients. Toss to mix.

PER SERVING: 472 cal, 17 g pro, 79 g car, 6 g fiber, 11 g fat (1 g sat fat), 0 mg chol, 885 mg sod

TIP After rinsing the beans and draining the corn in a colander, leave them there and drain the pasta over them so they can be warmed and all be returned to the pot at once.

Linguine with Roasted Vegetables

SERVES 6 • TOTAL TIME: 45 MIN

1½ lb plum tomatoes, cut in ¾-in. chunks

2 large zucchini (about 1¼ lb), quartered lengthwise, cut crosswise in ¾-in. pieces

1 yellow squash (about 6 oz), quartered lengthwise, cut crosswise in ¾-in. pieces

2 red bell peppers, cut in ½-in. pieces

1 medium red onion, coarsely chopped

3 Tbsp olive oil

1½ Tbsp minced garlic

1 tsp salt

½ tsp freshly ground pepper

1 lb linguine or spaghetti pasta

½ cup grated Parmesan cheese

⅓ cup chopped basil or parsley

GARNISH: grated Parmesan cheese

1. Adjust oven racks to divide oven in thirds. Preheat to 450°F. Have ready 2 rimmed baking sheets.

2. Bring a large pot of lightly salted water to a boil.

3. Put first 9 ingredients in a large bowl. Toss to mix and coat. Spread in baking sheets. Roast, switching position of pans once, 20 to 25 minutes until vegetables are tender.

4. Meanwhile, stir pasta into the boiling water and cook as package directs.

5. Remove and reserve ½ cup pasta cooking water. Drain pasta; return to pot. Add vegetables, scraping baking pans with a rubber spatula to include any juices, reserved cooking water, the cheese and basil or parsley. Toss to mix. Sprinkle with grated Parmesan cheese if desired.

PER SERVING: 437 cal, 16 g pro, 71 g car, 5 g fiber, 11 g fat (2 g sat fat), 5 mg chol, 794 mg sod

Pasta with Spring Vegetables

SERVES 4 • TOTAL TIME: ABOUT 35 MIN

12 oz cellentani pasta (short corkscrews)

1 box (10 oz) frozen petite green peas

2 tsp olive oil

1 lb asparagus, wood ends snapped off, spears cut in 2-in. pieces

1 medium (8 oz) yellow summer squash, cut in half lengthwise, then crosswise in ½-in. pieces

8 oz sugar-snap peas, ends trimmed

1 Tbsp minced garlic

1 pt (12 oz) grape tomatoes

1 tsp salt

½ tsp pepper

1 Tbsp cornstarch

1½ cups chicken broth

3 scallions, thinly sliced

Grated peel and juice from 1 lemon

Garnish: grated Parmesan cheese

1. Bring a large pot of lightly salted water to a boil. Add pasta and cook as package directs, adding peas 3 minutes before pasta is done. Drain and return to pot.

2. Meanwhile, heat a large deep skillet over medium-high heat. Add oil and heat until hot but not smoking. Add asparagus, squash and snap peas. Sauté, stirring often, 3 minutes or until almost crisp-tender. Stir in garlic, tomatoes, salt and pepper. Cook 2 minutes or until tomatoes begin to release their juices.

3. Stir cornstarch into broth until blended. Add to skillet and simmer 1 to 2 minutes or until slightly thickened.

4. Add vegetables, scallions, lemon peel and juice to pasta; toss to mix and coat. Sprinkle servings with grated Parmesan cheese.

PER SERVING: 328 cal, 14 g pro, 61 g car, 6 g fiber, 4 g fat (1 g sat fat), 0 mg chol, 574 mg sod

Asian-Style Pasta Salad

SERVES 4 • TOTAL TIME: 55 MIN

2¼ cups broccoli florets

2 cups cauliflower florets

1 yellow bell pepper, cut in strips

1⅓ cups (4 oz) mushrooms,
cut in half

2 Tbsp olive oil

½ tsp salt

¼ tsp pepper

1 pkg (9 oz) fresh linguine pasta

½ cup bottled red wine vinaigrette

2 Tbsp reduced-sodium soy sauce

1 Tbsp minced fresh ginger

2 tsp minced garlic

½ cup packed basil leaves,
cut in thin strips

⅓ cup unsalted roasted peanuts

1. Preheat oven to 425°F. Put vegetables, mushrooms, oil, salt and pepper in a large bowl; toss to mix. Spread vegetables evenly in a single layer in a roasting pan or on 2 rimmed baking sheets. Roast, stirring once, 25 minutes or until vegetables are lightly browned and tender.

2. Meanwhile, cook pasta in a large pot of lightly salted boiling water as package directs. Mix vinaigrette, soy sauce, ginger and garlic in a large serving bowl.

3. Drain pasta well. Add to serving bowl and toss to coat. Stir in roasted vegetables and basil until well mixed. Sprinkle servings with peanuts.

PER SERVING: **468 cal, 16 g pro, 52 g car, 6 g fiber, 23 g fat (3 g sat fat), 47 mg chol, 1,093 mg sod**

Cold Peanut-Noodle Salad

SERVES 6 • TOTAL TIME: 20 MIN

8 oz thin linguine pasta

DRESSING

⅔ cup bottled Thai-style peanut sauce

2 Tbsp *each* cider vinegar and water

1 tsp minced garlic

1 lb (8 cups) Chinese cabbage, shredded

½ English seedless (hothouse) cucumber, quartered lengthwise and thinly sliced crosswise (2 cups)

2 medium carrots, shredded (1½ cups)

⅓ cup *each* sliced scallions and chopped cilantro

¼ cup chopped salted dry-roasted peanuts

1. Bring a large pot of lightly salted water to a boil. Add pasta; cook as package directs. Drain in a colander and rinse under running cold water until cool. Drain well.

2. Meanwhile, mix Dressing ingredients in a large serving bowl. Add cabbage, cucumber, carrots, scallions and cilantro; toss to mix. Add cooled pasta and toss to mix and coat. Sprinkle servings with peanuts.

PER SERVING: **289 cal, 10 g pro, 44 g car, 6 g fiber, 8 g fat (1 g sat fat), 0 mg chol, 499 mg sod**

Orecchiette Alla Rustica

SERVES 6 • TOTAL TIME: 25 MIN

1 lb orecchiette pasta

2 Tbsp olive oil

3 large cloves garlic, thinly sliced

1 can (15 oz) cannellini beans, not drained

⅓ cup pitted Kalamata olives, cut in half

½ cup chopped fresh parsley

½ cup diced bottled roasted red pepper

Freshly ground pepper to taste

¼ cup grated Romano cheese

1. Cook pasta in a large pot of lightly salted boiling water as package directs. Drain, reserving ½ cup cooking water.

2. Meanwhile, heat oil in a large, deep skillet over medium heat. Add garlic; sauté just until golden. Immediately add beans with their liquid, the olives, about ½ the parsley and all the roasted pepper. Stir to mix, then cook until hot.

3. Add cooking water to skillet. Add pasta to skillet along with remaining parsley and a few twists of black pepper. Toss to mix and coat. Sprinkle with Romano cheese.

PER SERVING: 419 cal, 14 g pro, 70 g car, 5 g fiber, 9 g fat (2 g sat fat), 3 mg chol, 609 mg sod

Bow-Ties with Spinach & Cherry Tomatoes

SERVES 6 • TOTAL TIME: 25 MIN • SERVE AT ROOM TEMPERATURE

12 oz bow-tie (farfalle) pasta

4 Tbsp extra-virgin olive oil

1 Tbsp minced garlic

1 bag (10 oz) fresh spinach, tough stems removed, leaves torn bite-size

½ tsp *each* salt and pepper

1 pt (12 oz) cherry tomatoes, halved or quartered if large

½ cup pine nuts or slivered almonds, toasted

¾ cup shredded Parmesan cheese

1. Bring a large pot of lightly salted water to a boil. Add pasta; cook as package directs.

2. Meanwhile, heat 1 Tbsp oil in a large skillet over medium heat. Add ½ the garlic; sauté 1 minute, or until golden. Add ½ the spinach and ¼ tsp each salt and pepper; sauté 1 minute, or until spinach wilts. Add remaining spinach and cook until wilted. Remove to a plate.

3. Add remaining 3 Tbsp oil and remaining garlic to skillet. Sauté until garlic is golden. Add tomatoes and remaining ¼ tsp each salt and pepper. Cook 1 minute, or until tomatoes start to release their juices. Set aside.

4. Drain pasta in a colander and rinse under running cold water until cool, then drain well.

5. Put all ingredients in a large bowl. Toss gently to mix.

PER SERVING: 416 cal, 15 g pro, 47 g car, 3 g fiber, 19 g fat (4 g sat fat), 8 mg chol, 607 mg sod

Linguine with Fresh Tomatoes & Tofu

SERVES 6 • TOTAL TIME: 30 MIN

1 lb linguine or spaghetti pasta

4 large ripe tomatoes, cut in chunks

½ cup fresh basil, chopped

3 Tbsp olive oil

2 Tbsp minced garlic

½ tsp *each* salt and pepper

1 pkg (14 oz) firm tofu, drained, patted dry and cut in ¾-in. cubes

1 bag (10 oz) fresh spinach, tough stems removed, leaves coarsely chopped

GARNISH: grated Parmesan cheese

1. Cook pasta in a large pot of lightly salted boiling water as package directs; drain, reserving ⅓ cup cooking water. Return pasta to pot.

2. While pasta cooks, stir tomatoes, basil, 1 Tbsp each oil and garlic, and the salt and pepper in a bowl to mix.

3. Heat remaining 2 Tbsp oil in a large nonstick skillet over medium-high heat. Add tofu and sauté 4 to 5 minutes until lightly golden. Add remaining 1 Tbsp garlic; sauté 30 seconds until aromatic. Add spinach and 1 Tbsp water. Cover and cook 2 to 3 minutes until wilted.

4. Toss pasta with tomato and tofu mixtures and up to ⅓ cup reserved cooking water to loosen pasta. Serve with Parmesan cheese if desired.

PER SERVING: **433 cal, 18 g pro, 67 g car, 6 g fiber, 11 g fat (2 g sat fat), 0 mg chol, 248 mg sod**

Fusilli with Tomatoes & Mozzarella

SERVES 6 • TOTAL TIME: 30 MIN • SERVE AT ROOM TEMPERATURE

8 oz fusilli pasta

2 cups small broccoli florets

2 Tbsp *each* olive oil and rice vinegar

6 sun-dried tomatoes, chopped

1 clove garlic, minced

½ tsp *each* salt and pepper

8 oz (about 1 medium tomato) *each* red and yellow tomatoes, diced

8 oz mozzarella cheese, diced

½ cup pitted Kalamata olives, coarsely chopped

1 cup basil leaves, stacked and cut in narrow strips

GARNISH: grated Parmesan cheese

1. Bring a large pot of lightly salted water to a boil. Add pasta; cook as package directs, stirring in broccoli for last minute of cooking time. Drain pasta and broccoli, rinse under running cold water until cool, then set aside to drain.

2. Meanwhile, whisk oil, vinegar, sun-dried tomatoes, garlic, salt and pepper in a large bowl until well blended. Add tomatoes, mozzarella cheese, olives and cooled pasta. Toss to mix and coat. Sprinkle servings with basil. Add Parmesan cheese if desired.

PER SERVING: 510 cal, 16 g pro, 42 g car, 4 g fiber, 32 g fat (9 g sat fat), 33 mg chol, 1,665 mg sod

Penne with Chard & Pine Nuts

SERVES 6 • TOTAL TIME: 30 MIN

3 tsp olive oil

⅓ cup pine nuts

1 lb penne pasta

3 large cloves garlic, slivered

1¼ lb red Swiss chard (or a mix of white-, yellow-and red-stemmed chards), stems cut in 1-in. pieces; leaves stacked and cut crosswise in ribbons

1 cup chicken broth

½ tsp salt

½ cup oil-marinated sun-dried tomatoes, drained, cut in narrow strips

1 Tbsp balsamic vinegar

GARNISH: shredded Parmesan cheese

1. Bring a large pot of lightly salted water to a boil.

2. Heat 1 tsp of the oil in a large nonstick skillet over medium-high heat. Add pine nuts; sauté 2 to 3 minutes until toasted. Remove to a small bowl.

3. Stir penne into boiling water. Cook, stirring occasionally, as package directs.

4. Meanwhile, heat remaining 2 tsp oil in same skillet over medium-high heat. Add garlic; sauté 1 minute or until fragrant. Add chard stems, broth and salt. Cover and cook 1 to 2 minutes until crisp-tender. Add chard leaves, cover and, stirring once, cook 4 to 5 minutes until wilted.

5. Drain pasta and return to pot; toss with chard, pine nuts, tomatoes and vinegar. Pour into serving bowl. Sprinkle servings with Parmesan cheese.

PER SERVING: 433 cal, 14 g pro, 64 g car, 4 g fiber, 14 g fat (2 g sat fat), 0 mg chol, 1,256 mg sod

Stovetop Ziti

SERVES 6 • TOTAL TIME: 25 MIN

1 lb ziti pasta

1 bag (12 oz) broccoli florets

SAUCE

1 jar (26 oz) marinara sauce

1 cup skim ricotta cheese

4 oz part-skim mozzarella cheese, diced

⅓ cup chopped fresh parsley

¼ cup grated Parmesan cheese

1. Cook pasta in a large pot of lightly salted boiling water as package directs, adding broccoli 4 minutes before pasta is done.

2. Mix marinara sauce and about ½ the ricotta in a large saucepan. Cook over medium-low heat until hot.

3. Drain pasta and broccoli; return to pot. Add sauce mixture; toss to mix and coat. Immediately add mozzarella and about ½ the parsley and Parmesan. Stir until mozzarella melts.

4. Transfer to serving bowl; sprinkle with remaining parsley and Parmesan. Top with dollops of remaining ricotta.

PER SERVING: 478 cal, 25 g pro, 74 g car, 5 g fiber, 10 g fat (3 g sat fat), 14 mg chol, 1,257 mg sod

CHOOSING PASTA

Certain pastas are suited to certain sauces. Delicate capellini (angel-hair pasta) and a hearty, thick sauce are a poor match, but the same sauce could be tastily caught in the ridges or cups of a shorter, sturdier pasta. A pasta is suggested in each recipe, but others with similar shapes may be substituted.

Tortellini Primavera

SERVES: 4 • TOTAL TIME: 20 MIN

1 pkg (20 oz) refrigerated three-cheese tortellini

1 bag (1 lb) frozen sugar-snap stir-fry, thawed, large sugar snaps halved, if desired

1 jar (16 oz) creamy Alfredo sauce

1. Bring a large pot of lightly salted water to a boil. Add tortellini; cook as package directs, adding vegetables 2 minutes before pasta is done. Cook until tortellini and vegetables are tender. Drain in a colander.

2. Pour Alfredo sauce into pasta pot; cook over low heat until hot. Remove from heat; add pasta and vegetables and toss to mix and coat.

PER SERVING: **636 cal, 22 g pro, 76 g car, 6 g fiber, 20 g fat (12 g sat fat), 126 mg chol, 1,486 mg sod**

Photo Credits

Copyright © 2008 Filipacchi
Publishing, a division of Hachette
Filipacchi Media U.S., Inc.

First published in 2008 in the
United States of America by
Filipacchi Publishing
1633 Broadway
New York, NY 10019

Woman's Day is a registered
trademark of Hachette Filipacchi
Media U.S., Inc.

Design: Patricia Fabricant
Proofreading: Jennifer Ladonne
Production: Ed Barredo

ISBN 10: 1-933231-45-9
ISBN 13: 978-1-933231-45-7

Library of Congress
Control Number: 2008924232

Printed in China